Joseph Benson Gilder, James Russell Lowell

Impressions of Spain

Joseph Benson Gilder, James Russell Lowell

Impressions of Spain

ISBN/EAN: 9783337228903

Printed in Europe, USA, Canada, Australia, Japan

Cover: Foto ©Andreas Hilbeck / pixelio.de

More available books at **www.hansebooks.com**

IMPRESSIONS OF SPAIN

JAMES RUSSELL LOWELL

COMPILED BY

JOSEPH B. GILDER

WITH AN INTRODUCTION BY

A. A. ADEE

BOSTON AND NEW YORK
HOUGHTON, MIFFLIN AND COMPANY
The Riverside Press
1899

COPYRIGHT, 1899
BY
JOSEPH B. GILDER

Entered at Stationers' Hall, London

Prefatory Note

IT was over twenty-one years ago that the late James Russell Lowell arrived in Madrid as American Minister at the Spanish Court; yet no clearer insight into the state of affairs in Spain at the present day can be had, than is to be obtained from the reading of his official despatches to the Secretary of State at Washington. By knowledge of the history and the language of the country, he was exceptionally equipped for the mission to which President Hayes appointed him, and in a comparatively short time he had acquainted himself with the social and political conditions then prevalent, so that his comments on men and measures are invaluable to anyone desirous of tracing the causes of conditions prevalent to-day. To read Washington Irving's despatches of fifty years ago and Mr. Lowell's of thirty years later, is to be struck by the similarity of the conditions they reveal, and also by the close resemblance between the conditions in 1845 and 1878 and those of the present year of grace.

Mr. Lowell's first despatch from Spain is dated Monday, 20 Aug., 1877. It notes his arrival at Madrid on the preceding Tuesday, and that Mr. A. A. Adee, "our *Chargé d'Affaires,* of whose zealous kindness I cannot say too much," met him at the frontier, and promptly arranged for his own audience of leave-taking and Mr. Lowell's audience of reception on Saturday, Aug. 18.[1] "At the request of Señor Silvela, Minister of State, the Minister of the Interior very courteously placed at our disposal the

---

[1] Mr. Adee, the beginning of whose service in the State Department antedated this episode by several years, has been since 1886 Second Assistant Secretary of State.

Prefatory Note

private travelling carriage of Señor Cánovas del Castillo, who is at present absent from Madrid."

Arrived at La Granja, where the Court was summering, our Minister was kept waiting twenty minutes beyond the hour appointed for his audience with the King. The Introducer apologised, and Mr. Lowell said that he was personally satisfied, but that it should be remembered that it was not he "but the United States that were kept waiting." It transpired that the King had been waiting all the time in the audience chamber, and it was then the Minister's turn to apologise, which he accordingly did. During their brief stay at La Granja, both Mr. Lowell and Mr. Adee were treated by the King and his suite with marked courtesy, one of the pleasantest features of their sojourn being a dinner *en famille* with the royal family.

Mr. Lowell's official correspondence teems with references to and illustrations of Spain's good-will toward the United States. One evidence of this was her enthusiastic reception of Gen. Grant ; another, her refusal to impose retaliatory duties when a special tonnage tax had been imposed by us on Spanish vessels entering our ports ; others still were furnished by the gift of testimonials to American officers who had saved Spanish lives or property. On 1 Feb., 1878, Mr. Lowell wrote, in reference to the case of the whaling schooners *Ellen Rizpah*, *Rising Sun*, and *Edward Lee* : "The Spanish Government has acted with extraordinary promptness in the matter, if I may judge by the experience of my colleagues here, thus giving a further proof of its disposition to maintain friendly relations with the United States." Again, on 14 March, 1879, he acknowledged the receipt, in behalf of the Historical Society of St. Louis, of a photograph of King Alfonso with autograph below, "set in a very handsome frame of iron enamelled with gold and silver—a species of work peculiar to Spain."

Whereas many if not all of Washington Irving's despatches were written in his own handwriting throughout, all but three of Mr. Lowell's are in the handwriting of the secretary, bearing only the Minister's signature. On these three occasions the necessity of being his own secretary was imposed by his own kindness in granting special holidays to Mr. Dwight Reed, for whose health and happiness he shows a generous solicitude.

The letters which have been chosen for reproduction here are those in which our Minister describes the domestic politics of Spain; the King's first marriage, at the age of twenty-one, to his cousin Mercedes; the attempt upon his life; his bereavement; and his marriage to the Austrian Archduchess, Maria Cristina.

J. B. G.

CONTENTS

	INTRODUCTION	3
I.	THE DOMESTIC POLITICS OF SPAIN	23
II.	THE KING'S FIRST MARRIAGE	53
III.	THE DEATH OF QUEEN MERCEDES	75
IV.	ATTEMPTED ASSASSINATION OF THE KING	87
V.	GENERAL GRANT'S VISIT TO SPAIN	95
VI.	THE KING'S SECOND MARRIAGE	101
	INDEX	105

INTRODUCTION

Impressions of Spain

Introduction

A PHILOSOPHER, and in particular a genial one, shrewd to observe, and yet indulgent to, the foibles of his fellows, whom he surveys in the light of an amused and charitable introspection of his own nature, is apt to make a good diplomatist. Of this type was Franklin, the precursor of a distinguished line of American representatives at foreign courts taken from the walks of letter-craft. High in the ranks of these stood Lowell.

When, therefore, the relations of our country to Spain had reached a stage of comparative repose; when, after long turmoil and change, regular in its very inconstancy, the Celtiberian nation had wiped out old scores at home, pacified its unruly province beyond the sea, and addressed itself to the cultivation of civil well-being and progress, it was entirely fitting that our Government should turn from the employment of soldier-diplomatists like Sickles, and wily masters of profoundest jurisprudence like Cushing, as its envoys, and revert to the policy which, in 1842, on the eve of the girl-queen Isabel's assumption of the reins of government in her own thirteen-year-old right, had prompted the selection of Washington Irving as Minister to the Court of San Fernando.

Sickles and Cushing had borne the heat and burden of the long diplomatic campaign that opened with the Cuban revolution of 1868 and closed with the establishment of the judicial rights of our citizens in Spain and its insular possessions, by the signature of the Cushing-Calderon protocol in January, 1877. During most of these nine years the political aspect of Spain had been kaleidoscopic. From the downfall and flight of Isabel II., September 30, 1868, to the restoration of the Bourbon dynasty in the person of her son, Alfonso XII., the land had seen its governments come and depart like shadows, its fields harried by the wars of the Carlists and the communists, and Cuba, the boasted Ever Faithful Island, wasted by the ten years' rebellion of Yara. To the provisional triumvirate of Prim, Serrano, and Topete, which took hold of power on Isabel's dethronement, succeeded the regency of Serrano, under which a new monarchical constitution was framed, and the unlucky search for an exotic king begun.

The candidacy of Hohenzollern having served for naught save to set France and Germany at war, more expedient counsels prevailed in the election and enthronement of Amadeo of Savoy at the beginning of 1870.

| 6 | Impressions of Spain |

Introduction

Despite his sturdy devotion to the tenets of constitutional rule and his undying honesty of purpose in all that becomes the man of honour and the stainless monarch, the Italian prince's alienship was a fatal bar to his conquest of the love of an intensely national race, so that at the last, disheartened by the hopelessness of the task, and confronted by the need of an arbitrary dissolution of a hostile parliament and a resort to the traditional electoral methods of Castile to prop up a tottering power by the facile return of a subservient Córtes, Amadeo abdicated on February 11, 1873. The Senate and Chamber of Deputies, by an act of sheer usurpation, dissolved their separate constitutional existence, and declared themselves as forming in common union a constituent assembly to frame a government as the self-appointed delegates of the people. The short-lived republic was the outcome. Its first president, that grandly incorruptible statesman Estanislao Figueras, was succeeded in mid-

June by Francisco Pi y Margall, a man of dreamy theories and amiable lack of grip; on July 18th by Nicolas Salmeron, the most practical of the fleeting line; and on September 7th by Emilio Castelar, the orator, whose rule was troublous enough. To the remittent agony of the Carlist rebellion, which rose anew to confront the young republic, had been added the cantonal risings of July, when the southern and eastern provinces and even isolated towns proclaimed independent statehood and clamoured for a federation. To oppose this movement, due as much to Castelar's former teachings as to any other motive, it became necessary to revive the eras of militarism, from which Spain had already too long suffered. On September 21st, the Assembly suspended its sittings until January, conferring the supreme dictatorship, during the interval, upon Castelar's council of ministers. On January 2d, Castelar resigned his office to the assembled Córtes and invited a vote of confidence, which was overwhelmingly rejected. The next night, January 3, 1874, while the Assembly was deliberating the choice of still another president, the republic fell by the *coup d'état* of General Pavia, who set up the presidency-dictatorship of Serrano in its stead. A year later, the shards and scraps of the political kaleidoscope took a fresh arrangement through the rude jolt given by Marshal Martinez de Campos, who, on December 29, 1874, set up the Bourbon standard at Sagunto, and, backed by the whole army, placed Alfonso XII. on the throne, with Cánovas del Castillo as regent until His Majesty should return from his school-days' exile.

Throughout all these changes the people of Spain seem to have been the first to acquiesce, as they were the last to be consulted by the metropolitan makers of regents, presidents, and kings. Like their Gallic neighbours, anything was welcome to the masses that might not bode increased strife and taxation, and each successive administration took office with the reassuring promise of reform and stability. Hence, as Mr. Cushing wrote of the accession of Alfonso, "it did not appear at all extraordinary to the Spaniards, on waking up, to find that the republic had vanished and the monarchy returned with the dramatic celerity of a change of scenery at the opera. . . . The people are beginning to conceive that *revolutionism*, as a principle or theory of government, is the climax of nonsense and absurdity, seeing that it is to convert the desperate remedy for a mortal disease into the daily food of its life, and thus, under pretence of curing the occasional ills of the body politic, to condemn it to inevitable death and dissolution. In a word, weary of empiricism, demagogy, and anarchy, Spain seeks refuge once more in the hoped-for repose of its traditional institutions of religion and hereditary monarchy."[1]

---

[1] Mr. Cushing to Mr. Fish, January 5, 1875.

Impressions of Spain

Introduction

In a little more than six years Spain had endured as many changes in the form of government, having tried the provisional committee, the regency, the elective monarchy, the republic, the dictatorship, and the restored hereditary monarchy. During the ten and a half months of the republic, five presidents had been installed, not to mention the sixteen hours' phantom, Pedregal, whose insignificance set Madrid agape, and who retired before the street clamour "Quien es Pedregal?" without even forming a cabinet. Carlism and cantonalism had wasted the land and burdened its people with dread and debt. The Cuban war still dragged on, in spite of endless sacrifice of life and treasure and the concession of emancipation and political reforms. As worse could hardly be expected to come, the revived monarchy under a native sovereign might at least be a presage of better things, such as a union of the contending internal factions of the realm, and an era of tranquillity and dedication to normal pursuits. The hope proved not wholly vain. The next few years saw the country in peace at home, while across the seas the fires of insurrection in Cuba were visibly waning before the peculiarly persuasive treatment of Martinez de Campos, who finally, in 1877, brought about the truce of Zanjon.

It was under these favourable conditions that Mr. Lowell went to Spain in August, 1877, there to remain until his transfer to the London mission in January, 1880. No grave international responsibility confronted him. The only cloud on the good relations of the United States and Spain, the *Virginius* quarrel, had been dispelled through the settlement effected by his predecessor. In the Spanish eye he came, not to continue the disputatious and aggressive diplomacy of Sickles and Cushing, but to revive the amiable traditions of Washington Irving's day. With the natural confusion of surnames on the paternal and maternal side, which in Castilian usage are combined in one double appellation, the leading government organ welcomed "the poet Russell, equally with the diplomatist Lowell." He was even familiarly greeted by some as "José Bighlow," with the hopeful anticipation that a fresh volume of dialectic verse might result from his Spanish experiences; while others, more lately informed, trusted that he would, from his Window, survey with kindly philosophic gaze the more lovable and human side of the Spanish character. I think he himself planned to leave some enduring record of his sojourn. His maturer mind did not gratefully accept the measure of intellectual power which a reversion to the aphoristic critical standard of John P. Robinson would have imposed. Possessing a singularly well-grounded acquaintance with the Castilian tongue and literature, he looked wistfully forward to revisiting the Spain of his youth, the land where the traditions of Fernando and Isabel still lingered, to associating in the flesh with modern Santa Teresas, Luis de Leons, Calderons, and Quevedos on a footing of close intimacy, and to collecting the matter for some great literary work. The Spain of to-day, unstable, frivolous, and wholly reminiscent, without the will or the physical power to revert to dimly remembered heights of greatness, was to be to him a sore disillusionment.

His reception was as congenial to his simple nature as it was flattering to his vanity as a writer. His induction to court life was not among the stately surroundings of the Palacio Real, but at the summer seat of San Ildefonso, the famed Granja. The monarch he met was a laughing boy, full of easy-going camaraderie, happy in the double flush of royal honours and of love's young witchery. His first court meal was an unconventional family dinner where the prattle of Alfonso and his cousin Mercedes overbore mere statecraft and political science. His first intimate associate was Manuel Silvela, the Minister for Foreign Affairs, an accomplished man of letters, more prone to discuss a play of Lope's than a commercial treaty, through whom he gained instant entrance into the charmed circle of the literati, and set up his court among them as an acknowledged leader. The friendship of Lowell for Silvela lasted throughout his mission. He was fortunate, too, in winning the close friendship of that keen-sighted statesman, Cánovas, not only by far the ablest of Spain's nineteenth-century leaders, but one of the foremost premiers of Europe, of whose political "omnipotence" he quaintly writes.

No great historical event marked the career of Spain during Lowell's stay. He witnessed, on January 23, 1878, the love-match of the boy-king with his girl-cousin Mercedes, a natural sequel to the love-making of the Granja family dinner of the preceding August. Five months later he, a sincere mourner among mourners, attended the funeral pageant of the young queen, who in her brief but sunny throne-life had by her sweetness and tact overcome the resentful distrust with which the people at first received the daughter of the disliked Montpensier, and won the love of a generous nation.[1] On November 29, 1879, he saw the union of Alfonso with that true-hearted and devoted wife and mother, the Archduchess Maria Christina of Austria, who, later, in 1886, after the young king's death, was to ascend the throne as dowager queen regent during the minority of the posthumous heir, Alfonso XIII., the present King of Spain. Betweenwhiles Lowell joined in the ceremonial congratulations to His Majesty upon his unharmed escape from the bullets of the

---

[1] For an account of the attractive personality of young Mercedes, see the reminiscences by Henrietta C. Dana entitled "A Queen at School," in *The Century* for April, 1878.

anarchists Moncasi and Otero. He duly advised the Department of State of all these happenings, investing each with the charm of his exquisite style. At times, lacking weightier matters of discourse, he did not disdain to rehearse gravely some passing tattle or whispered scandal of the court, or to relate some humorous incident, better fitted for the editorial fourth column of a metropolitan daily than for the shelves of a staid foreign office. His habit of making his departmental reports delightful reading is seen in the despatches reproduced in the following pages. Even the repulsive dryness of a negotiation for commercial reciprocity did not daunt him; he found in the Spanish presentation of the case the text for a homily on Castilian sensitiveness. All this shows how great a loser the world has been by Lowell's failure to make an ever-living book about Spain. Like many men to whom composition is a pastime and a delight, the Hamlet-like habit of putting off sober tasks to a more convenient season was uppermost, and, in his half-indolent, half-satiated enjoyment of what each day brought to him, he unconsciously adopted as his motto the Spanish saw he often quoted, *Mañana es otro dia* ("There is another day to-morrow"). His private letters to his intimates, some phrased in choice Castilian, had in them the meat and marrow of a dozen books.

Lowell wrote little of the domestic politics of Spain, perhaps appreciating the difficulty of making clear to an alien mind that which is and ever must be incomprehensible to the Castilians themselves, and none the less so to the alien observer. He hints as much in the exordium of the long despatch which follows. Necessarily lacking the knowledge of the true springs of national impulse deep down in the heart of the masses, he dealt with the surface indications, and analysed the character and motives of the men on top, whose peculiarities most caught his attention. He gave away no state secrets, for he had none to give. His kindly nature forbade any wounding comment or trenchant imputations,—for which unhappily there is as much room in Spain as in any other land whose latter-day history is made up of political drifts and eddies,—but with epigrammatic facility he has hit off personal traits and suggested personal motives, always speaking *ex cathedra* with the same lofty impartiality as though dissecting the bygone rivalries and intrigues of Athens or Rome. One can hardly fail to see that criticism like this is of all time ; that the puppets and the scene may change, while the action goes on; that, after all, the story and the moral are merely those of the world-old struggle between the ins and the outs; and that the winning by partisans of their master's good grace is, to quote Lowell's words, but the indifferent shifting of a cloud of gnats "from the head of one passer-by to that of another."

Analysis like this throws no light on the great problems of racial destiny. It cannot compute the cyclic movements of peoples. But it is charming reading all the same, as much so as a study from the essayist's Window at Cambridge.

A. A. ADEE.

1

THE DOMESTIC POLITICS OF SPAIN

I

THE DOMESTIC POLITICS OF SPAIN

26 August, 1878.

I HAVE always been chary of despatches concerning the domestic politics of Spain, because my experience has taught me that political prophets who make even an occasional hit, and that in their own country, where they are presumed to know the character of the people and the motives likely to influence them, are as rare as great discoverers in science. Such a conjunction of habitual observation with the faculty of instantaneous logic that suddenly precipitates the long accumulations of experience, whose angles may be measured and their classification settled, can hardly be expected

Outside Influences

of an observer in a foreign country. Its history is no longer an altogether safe guide, for, with the modern facility of intercommunication, influences from without continue to grow more and more directly operative ; and yet wherever, as in Spain, the people is almost wholly dumb, there is no means of judging how great the infiltration of new ideas may have been. Where there is no well-defined national consciousness with recognised organs of expression, there can be no public opinion, and therefore no way of divining what its attitude is likely to be under any given circumstances.

Spaniards especially have been so habituated to sudden changes and to revolutions that began in a corner that they are apt to reckon confidently on the probability of one. In what I shall say I shall not repeat what Spaniards have said to me, but shall give my own conclusions from a study of the press, and from what I have been able to gather from the impressions of intelligent foreigners who have been travelling in Spain, with favourable opportunities of learning what the state of feeling really is, at least in the large cities.

There are many parties, with more or less distinctly outlined principles or opinions; but the will, the ideas, the aspirations, I might almost say the very life, of all these is, I think, more completely in Spain than in most other countries, personified in certain leaders with whom selfish ambitions are apt, sooner or later, to take the place of principle, and whose partisans unconsciously substitute them for the interests of the country. It is almost always the probable action or inaction of certain leaders that the newspapers discuss, though there is no lack of ability for the treatment of more comprehensive questions. The concentration of all national life in the capital tends to intensify the personal rivalries, jealousies, and animosities of these leaders by the immediate contact of competitors,

A Multiplicity of Leaders

"Empleo-mania"

and by the sight of men in power who perhaps started from a lower level than themselves. If we add to this an unmistakable tinge of Orientalism, and a very large infusion in the upper and middle classes of the most intense, restless, aspiring, and unscrupulous blood of all, the Jewish, perhaps we should rather wonder at the moderation than the passion of Spanish politics. It should be remembered also that the Spanish people (the elections being a sham) have no regulated and constitutional method of expressing their will, and that repression has its natural result of intensifying the desires it thwarts, and not only of justifying the means by the end, but of gradually substituting the one for the other.

The *empleomania,* which is the dry-rot of Spain, as it threatens to become of the United States, supplies every leader with a momentarily devoted band of adherents, ready to transfer themselves at any moment to a more promising chief, as a cloud of gnats shifts indifferently from the head of one passer-by to that of another. There are always at least three pretenders to the seat of power—the ousted line of the royal family, the Conservatives, and the radical Republicans. Don Carlos is for the present out of the question, because he is out of funds, and the Republicans have no ostensible strength in the Córtes, so that the former cannot brew a civil war, nor the latter aspire to defeat, and so to change, the ministry by those parliamentary methods which are assumed to be in practice, and all the motions of which are performed with the gravity of Roman augurs. The parties which make any show in the Córtes are the *Moderados* (Tories), *Moderados-Históricos* (High Tories and Ultramontanes), and the *Constitucionalistas,* who demand the adoption of the more liberal constitution of 1869. These are all royalists of different shades, or profess to be so, though the last-named have decided repub-

Three Kinds of Royalists

No Opposition

lican leanings, and could easily reconcile themselves with a republic which should put them in power.

The government of Señor Cánovas, of course, permits and even favours the election as deputies of a few opponents who are harmless, like Señor Castelar; but real opposition in the Córtes there is none. By real opposition I mean one based on principle and with any chance of carrying through a single measure of its own, or defeating one of the government. This seems to be one of the chief dangers of Señor Cánovas's position, and that in two ways: first, by begetting that blind trust in absolute power which in the possessor of it insensibly substitutes will for reason; and, second, because legitimate discontent that is not supplied with safe vents will be sure to make or seek dangerous outlets.

The fact that all parties of the nominal opposition are announcing their intention, with more or less emphasis, to practise what is decorously called "a policy of abstention" at the approaching elections, shows that for the moment, at least, the actual government has the game in its own hands. The question for a looker-on is merely whether the wisest advantage is taken of the powerful hand.

So far as I can judge with my present means, Señor Cánovas del Castillo seems to me at present not only the ablest politician in Spain, but in many important respects capable also of being her most far-seeing statesman. He has the great advantage (especially rare here) of being familiar with history and with the great principles which underlie it. He is by far the strongest parliamentary debater in the Córtes, the only one who goes straight to the question and never wanders from it. Señor Castelar is no doubt more eloquent; but his speeches always, in my judgment, obscure his subject with a rainbow-tinted mist, through which the most familiar objects look strangely

Señor Cánovas del Castillo

Señor Cánovas's Weak Point

unreal. His principles of action (I might almost call them principles of diction) have always, like the goddess of Homer, a convenient cloud into which they withdraw at need from mortal apprehension. But if the use of speech be to move men rather than to persuade them, he is, I am ready to believe, the greatest of contemporary orators, and comparable with the greatest of any period, especially with Lamartine in 1848. He says many sensible, many wise things, but they seem with him rather acquired than intuitive.

The weak point, then, in Señor Cánovas's position is his omnipotence, for this, without omniscience to steady it, is almost sure to become headstrong and contemptuous of conciliation. He has, and justly, a very high conception of his own ability, and of his services to the country; but I think I have seen symptoms of the degeneration of this sense of his own value into a belief that he is indispensable. This is sometimes the most fatal dementia of those whom *Deus vult perdere.*

I am speaking of a country, it should be remembered, which has adopted constitutional forms, but has never acquired the habitude of constitutional procedure when shorter methods seem for the moment more effective or convenient. The policy of Señor Cánovas is, on the whole (under the convenient euphemism of liberal-conservative), a reactionary one, and seems in danger of becoming more so. This may be the result of a real conviction in his own mind resulting from the errors and excesses of the short-lived republic; or he may be acting on the belief that such a conviction is strong enough and general enough in the public mind to form the secure basis of a policy; or it may have had its origin in a miscalculation of the strength of the reactionary movement in France. In either case it is mistaking the eddy for the current. Either of these may be supposed to be the

An Administration in the Air

motive of Señor Cánovas, the politician. But I think that we may both charitably and probably assume a different one for Señor Cánovas, the statesman. I will suppose that he reasons thus: "The great need of the country is repose and a stable administration. These are the preliminary conditions of reform, a reform of which I see the need and wish the success as much as any man. The problem, therefore, is to establish a government liberal enough in form to keep the Republicans from rising, and repressive enough in fact to keep the Tories from plotting."

The objection to a policy which for the moment may neutralise both parties, but satisfies neither, is that, in military phrase, the administration which pursues it is in the air. It has no solid base and no reserves of strength. During his three years of power Señor Cánovas has failed to form a party. He has been governing by a league of incongruous factions which consented to unite upon him as the readiest temporary expedient, and will drop away from him the moment the leaders think they see a chance of realising their own special political opinions, or of getting into power without him. His cabinet is incongruous (as a cabinet of compromise cannot fail to be), and therefore weak, while all its mistakes are sure to be laid at the door of its chief.

Causes of Discontent

The dynasty, I hear from all quarters, and not from Spaniards alone, does not strike root. Discontent, mainly due to economic derangements, resulting sometimes from general causes, sometimes also, it is true, from unwise, unequal, or too often corrupt administration, is universal. Taxation is so excessive that in many provinces hundreds (the newspapers say thousands) of farms are abandoned to the tax-gatherer. The Biscayan provinces are full of resentment at the abolition of their ancient privileges, and against Señor Cánovas as the author of

The Middle Classes Republican

it. I need not say that in Spain, more than anywhere else, discontent is likely to take a political turn, which means, for the most part, a violent one. When the feeling is general, even though without definite object, it begets *pronunciamentos* by offering them the chances of success. Though, as I have said, the instincts (or perhaps I should say the habits) of absolutism are still predominant, yet the last forty years have made a great change in the Spanish people. The middle classes have become intelligent, rich, and conscious of their value and of the power which results from it. They would be content, or at any rate, quiet, under a constitutional monarchy, where the elections, the press, education, and religious belief were free ; but they are republicans in theory and in their habits of life.

In considering the chances of a change of ministries, another element is to be taken into consideration, and that is the personal preferences of the King. Señor Cánovas has been governing, it is true, by what seem to be parliamentary methods, and has the support of an apparent parliamentary majority. But the whole arrangement is artificial, and the majority represents no definite opinions either in the Córtes or the country, unless we understand by a definite opinion the determination to have no opinions at all. The supporters of Señor Cánovas look on him as a plank in shipwreck to which they are content to cling for the present, but every one of them with the hope or intention of making a bridge of it, one of these days. Intrigues are going on continually, and as the King, of course, has the right of dismissing and summoning ministers, these intrigues, as always hitherto in Spain, centre around the palace. It is true that theoretically the calling of new counsellors should follow a parliamentary defeat of the old; but as the majority in the Córtes is purely factitious, it can never play the part of a reality, and accord-

An Atmosphere of Intrigue

The King's Education

ingly it is very natural for one who is *out* and wishes to be *in* to argue, and not very hard to persuade himself, that the *sic volo, sic jubeo,* of the King is at least as good as that of Señor Cánovas.

The King is intelligent and well-meaning, but can hardly be expected at his age to take a very comprehensive view of politics. Ministerial writers are fond of pointing to the advantage he has had in an education of exile. But such an education has also its very great disadvantages. While it may enable him to know more of the world (though this is doubtful in the case of a prince), it has prevented his becoming acquainted with his own country. It has put him under personal obligations (such as no ruler should permit) to those who were faithful to him in evil days. It may have habituated him to intrigue, with all its dangerous and debasing consequences. His country may have come to seem a stake to be played for, rather than the noblest and most exacting of responsibilities.

A possible Solution

The newspapers have been discussing nearly all summer the possibilities and probabilities of a change, and what is called the *solucion Posada Herrera;* that is, the formation of a new cabinet, with that gentleman as its head, has been constantly cropping out, and in various quarters. I confess that I attached no great importance to it until the *Epoca*, a conservative paper hitherto Cánovist through thick and thin, took it up a few days ago, and published in the form of a correspondent's letter the report of a conversation with Señor Posada Herrera, in which, while expressing the greatest deference for Señor Cánovas del Castillo, he pointed out what he thought his mistakes of policy; thereby, of course, sketching by implication the course which a cabinet of his own selection would be likely to pursue. It is now whispered that the whole affair is an intrigue of the Duke

General Serrano's Attitude

of Sexto, governor of Don Alfonso when a boy, and now his *mayordomo mayor*, an office which brings him into continual and intimate contact with the King. . .

A far more important piece of news just beginning to be whispered, and to which I give more credit, is the reported going over of General Serrano (the Duke of La Torre) to the Republicans, under some arrangement with Sagasta, leader of the Constitutionalists. Serrano is said to retain his influence and popularity with the army; he has been regent; is a man who reminds one of Marshal MacMahon, but with more good sense and more sympathy with modern ideas. Meanwhile, as some confirmation of the Serrano-Sagasta rumour, Señor Castelar, who had given rise to very fierce newspaper polemics in the democratic press by a privately circulated letter of which I have a copy, is inculcating reconciliation and union through his special organ, *El Globo*.

Senor Cánovas is fertile in resources, and it remains to be seen what his course will be, and how much strength the *status quo* still has in the country through the fear of possible disorder. My own conclusion is that, sooner or later (perhaps sooner rather than later), the final solution will be a conservative republic like that of France. Should the experiment there go on prosperously a few years longer, should the French Senate become sincerely republican at the coming elections, the effect here could not fail to be very great, perhaps decisive. In one respect the Spanish people are better prepared for a republic than might at first sight be supposed. I mean that republican habits in their intercourse with each other are and have long been universal. Every Spaniard is a *caballero,* and every Spaniard can rise from the ranks to position and power. This also is in part, perhaps, an inheritance from the Mohammedan occupation of Spain. *Del rey ninguno abajo* is an ancient Spanish

Censorship of the Press

proverb implying the equality of all below the king. Manners, as in France, are democratic, and the ancient nobility here as a class are even more shadowy than the dwellers in the Faubourg St.-Germain.

In attacking Senor Cánovas, the opposition papers dwell upon the censorship of the press, upon the reëstablishment of monarchism under other names, and upon the onerous restrictions under which the free expression of thought is impossible. The ministerial organs reply to the first charge that more journals were undergoing suspension at one time during the Liberal administration of Señor Sagasta than now; and this is true. The fact is that no party, and no party leader, in Spain is capable of being penetrated with the truth—perhaps the greatest discovery of modern times—that freedom is good, above all, because it is safe. Señor Cánovas is doing only what any other Spaniard would do in his place; that is, endeavouring to suppress opinions which he believes to be mischievous. But of the impolitic extreme to which the principle is carried under his administration, though, I suspect, without his previous consent, the following fact may serve as an example:

Señor Manuel Merelo, professor in the Instituto del Cardenal Cisneros, published, in 1869, a compendium of Spanish history for the use of schools. In speaking of the revolution of 1868, he wrote: "It is said that the light conduct [*las liviandades*] of Queen Isabel II was one of the causes of this catastrophe." After an interval of nine years he has been expelled from his chair, and his book suppressed.

If any change should take place, which I confess I do not expect, but which in a country of personal government and pronunciamentos is possible to-morrow, I think the new administration will find that, with the best intentions in the world, a country which has been misgoverned for three cen-

The Ex-Queen's "Liviandades"

turies is not to be reformed in a day. At the same time I believe Spain to be making rapid advances toward the conviction that a reform is imperative and can only be accomplished by the good will and, above all, the good sense of the entire nation. There are strong prejudices and rooted traditions to be overcome, but with time and patience I believe that Spain will accomplish the establishment of free institutions under whatever form of government.

20 October, 1877.

In one of my late despatches (No. 10) I mentioned my belief that Spain was disposed to make a weapon of her commercial system. Whatever be the deliberate views of the government, it is quite certain, I think, from the tone of the press, that public opinion urges strongly in that direction. If Spain were richer and more powerful,—if she were as rich and powerful as, with her resources, she ought to be,—perhaps this would not be so, or at least not to the same degree; but, as it is, the national pride is sensitive in proportion to the country's decline in prosperity at home and consideration abroad, and pardonably enough seeks in the application of differential duties that which is denied in more noisy if less important fields.

If the armies and navies of Spain no longer weigh as once in the political scales of Europe, her custom-houses at least may continue to inspire the foreigner with a wholesome respect, and her scale of duties may still put her on a level with her most powerful rivals in diplomacy and war.

I am not condemning this as a weakness; for all national criticism in bulk is misleading and foolish, and I look upon the belief of Spaniards that Spain ought to be great and strong as the most promising agency of her future regeneration.

This sensitive nerve of theirs has just been jarred by the announcement, in a letter from Washington, that "by a decree of

"A Decree of the President"

the President, dated September 7, an additional tonnage duty of fifty cents the ton (making eighty cents in all) has been laid on all Spanish vessels entering American ports." I had no information whatever on the subject, nor could any be found in such files of American papers as the legation possessed. I knew, of course, that "a decree of the President" showed an ignorance of our Constitution worthy of certain English ministers of fifteen years ago, and that the so-called "decree" could be nothing more than the putting in force by the Secretary of the Treasury of some provision in a previous act of Congress which he was authorised to do upon a certain contingency. Under the circumstances, I was not sure whether I ought not to think the whole story an invention. But as, whether true or not, it was making much excitement here, I thought best to inquire by telegraph, as I did two days ago. I found the Spanish government as much in the dark as I was.

The opposition press naturally enough made the most of the affair, and advocated immediate retaliation, hinting at a certain want of national spirit in the ministry. The ministerial papers, no better informed than the rest of the world on a subject about which nobody knew anything whatever, were, of course, unwilling to be behindhand in patriotism, and equally so to advocate any inconsiderate action. Both parties are now agreed in counselling that an equivalent tonnage duty should be laid upon American vessels to the Peninsula and Balearic Islands. The Madrid Society of Political Economy, which is spoken of as a body of much weight, has also appointed a committee to wait upon the ministry with a similar recommendation. Thus all parties seem to be agreed that only one course is consistent with the dignity and interest of Spain. This is the more natural as the protectionist party is powerful here, and the ablest of the opposition journals, the

Señor Silvela's Anxiety

Imparcial, is a fervent believer in the virtues of a high tariff. I ought to add that the tone of all the newspapers I have seen has been perfectly dispassionate and courteous.

In the absence of any more exciting political topic, this piece of news from America assumed a somewhat disproportionate importance and gave some uneasiness to the ministry, who were sincerely anxious to preserve the most friendly relations with the United States. The minister of state at once made inquiries by telegraph of the Spanish representative at Washington. His answer was that such a tonnage duty had been laid on Spanish vessels, and that he would send further particulars in writing.

Yesterday Mr. Silvela called upon me, and it was evident that the affair was giving him a great deal of annoyance. He repeated what I have already told you concerning the attitude of the press and the current of public opinion. He said that the ministry

were exceedingly reluctant to adopt any
measure of retaliation, and would not do so
unless their hands were forced by consider-
ations of policy which they could not dis-
regard. He again spoke of the great effort
they had made to promote friendly feeling
on the part of the United States in the pay-
ment of the indemnity in cash, when every
peseta—nay, every real—was a matter of
consequence to them, and when they were
making every possible exertion and sacrifice
to put their finances in a more tolerable
condition, even to the extent, he added,
with a smile, of laying a tax of twenty-five
per cent. on all official salaries. He wished
me to observe the analogy between their
situation and that of the United States
immediately after the Civil War. . . .
He urged the advantage to both Spain and
the United States of a treaty of commerce
and navigation, for which the occasion was
favourable. . . .

I should not have thought it worth while

Spanish Sensitiveness

to write at so much length about this matter, were it not that it occupies public attention here, and might, I think, if left unexplained, give a wrong impression of the feelings and intentions of the President toward Spain. It must be remembered that in spite of the advances made by Spain toward an understanding of true political principles,—and I think they are great,—the old tradition of personal government is still rooted in men's habits of thought, and this leads insensibly to an attribution of motives and designs which have often no foundation in reason or reality. At the same time, by crediting the President with powers and functions which do not belong to him, false expectations are raised as to what he may do *motu proprio*, and the necessary disappointment of these produces that irritation which is not possible against an abstraction. Spain, also, in the peculiar difficulties of her position, is sensitive, and perhaps suspicious, beyond what would be natural under other circumstances. I cannot but believe it the wish of the President that every obstacle to a good understanding which can honourably be removed may be removed,[1] and that every reciprocation of good feeling which can properly be made may be made, as for the common interest of both countries. In addition to what Mr. Silvela asked me to remember, I could not help recalling that of the western European powers certainly none fulfilled her obligations toward us during our Civil War more faithfully than Spain.

20 May, 1879.

I have the honour to report that we have a new minister of state in place of the Marquis of Molins, who resumes his former post as ambassador at Paris. This is the Duke of Tetuan, nephew of the celebrated O'Donnell, and who has been minister at Lisbon and Vienna.

I think there is every reason to be satis-

---
[1] The duty was removed by President Hayes.

An Amiable Minister

fied with the change. The duke is a very amiable man, with excellent intentions, who told me at our first official reception that he "should try to be a continuation of Mr. Silvela." Nothing would be more satisfactory to the whole diplomatic body here than this.

I feel quite sure that my official relations with the new minister will be agreeable, and that he will do for us whatever a person in his position can. I said to him that I thought the importance of the friendship of the United States to Spain was hardly so fully understood here as it should be. He said in reply: "I think *I* appreciate its value," adding, with a smile, "my wife was a Cuban."

II

THE KING'S FIRST MARRIAGE

II

THE KING'S FIRST MARRIAGE

13 December, 1877.

YESTERDAY the diplomatic body received official communication of the intended marriage of the King with his cousin the Princess Mercedes, daughter of the Duke of Montpensier. Thus the famous Spanish marriages of thirty years ago, which helped to dethrone Louis Philippe, have borne fruit at last, and one of his grandchildren will share, though she cannot occupy, the throne of Spain. The result is not precisely what was intended, but comes nearer to being so than mortal plans or prophecies commonly do. The King is very intelligent and performs all his cere-

A Love
Match

monial functions with grace. The Princess is good looking, of suitable age, and has been well and sensibly brought up. The match is said, by those best entitled to know, to be one of affection on both sides, and so seldom does love contrive to win his way into a palace under any disguise, that I am quite ready to believe he has managed it at last. Malice, no doubt, would contrive to find ground in this case also for some suspicion of a dynastic arrangement, based on the hope of an Orleanist restoration in France by the management of the Duke of Broglie. It is so hard, however, to make out the truth of history, even after it has been written with seeming clearness in events, that it is hardly worth while attempting to divine the precise bearing and significance of such parts of it as do not contrive to get written at all. If any such hope conduced to the present matrimonial arrangement, it has been apparently baffled by the admirable self-restraint of the French people. It would certainly have been a very natural and even praiseworthy hope, if ever entertained, from a Spanish point of view, but that it had any influence at all in the affair is nothing more than a surmise that has sometimes suggested itself to my mind during the last few months. At any rate it is a truce, not a peace, that has been arrived at in France, and that as the result rather of a drawn battle than of a victory.

The royal wedding is to take place on the 23d of next month, with as much as possible of traditional Spanish ceremony and modes of public rejoicing. Meanwhile, as a natural preliminary, the price of every thing has doubled in Madrid, and the city is reckoning, in what is generally called by Europeans a very American spirit, on the profit to be made out of the strangers who will be tempted into its net.

Before this reaches you, you will doubtless have received an official communi-

Congratulating the King.

cation through the Spanish Minister at Washington.

3 February, 1878.

Immediately on receiving the President's telegram congratulating the King upon his approaching marriage, I communicated the substance of it to the Minister of State and asked for an audience that I might present it in person to His Majesty. On Monday (the 21st ultimo) accordingly I was received by King Alfonso in private audience and delivered my message, at the same time adding that it gave me particular pleasure to be the bearer of it. The King in reply desired me to convey to the President his great pleasure in receiving this expression of sympathy from the Chief Magistrate of a people with which he wished always to maintain and draw closer the most friendly relations. A very gracefully turned compliment to the messenger followed.

The King, I may add, performs all these ceremonial parts of his function with a grace, tact and good humour which have struck me as indicating a singularly agile intelligence as well as an amiable character.

I think that this act of courtesy on the part of the President has really given pleasure here, and has not been entirely lost in the throng of special ambassadors who have been despatched hither with numerous suites to pay the royal compliments of the occasion.

As these special ambassadors had been received in public audience, I had some doubt whether I ought to consent, as being in this case the immediate representative of the President, to be received privately. But the time was too short for much consideration. The audience was to be at half-past one o'clock, and I received notice of it only the night before. Had it been a *letter* of the President, I should have insisted on its being received publicly. As it was, I thought it most prudent and graceful to admit the distinction between Ex-

Ministerial Misgivings

The Slow-Going Despatch Bag

traordinary Ambassadors sent with great pomp to bring gifts and decorations, and a mere Minister Plenipotentiary, especially as it would have otherwise been impossible to deliver the message at all before the wedding.

The difficulty was heightened by my having only just risen from a very severe attack of illness, which made it necessary for me to economise my strength in order to take any part at all in the ceremonies.

6 February, 1878.

In these days of newspaper enterprise, when everything that happens, ought to happen, or might have happened, is reported by telegraph to all quarters of the world, the slow-going despatch bag can hardly be expected to bring anything very fresh or interesting in regard to a public ceremonial which, though intended for political effect, had little political significance. The next-morning frames of fireworks are not inspiring except to the moralist, and Madrid is already quarrelling over the cost and mismanagement of a show for the tickets to which it was quarrelling a week ago. Yet a few words will not be out of place upon a royal holiday which but yesterday divided the attention of the world with the awful historical tragedy of the East and the momentous social problems which are looming in the West. Nowhere in the world could a spectacle have been presented which recalled so various, so far-reaching and in some respects so sublime associations, yet rendered depressing by a sense of anachronism, of decay, and of that unreality which is all the sadder for being gorgeous. The Roman amphitheatre *(panem et circenses)*, the united escutcheons from whose quartering dates the downfall of Saracenic civilization and dominion in Spain; the banners of Lepanto and of the Inquisition fading together into senile oblivion on the walls of the Atocha; the names and titles that

Gorgeous Unreality

A Dazzling Picture

recalled the conquest of western empires or the long defeat whose heroism established the independence of the United Provinces and proved that a confederacy of traders could be heroic; the stage-coaches, plumed horses, blazing liveries and running footmen of Louis Quatorze; the partisans of Philip III.'s body-guard, the three-cornered hats, white breeches and long black gaiters of a century ago, mingled pellmell with the French shakos and red trousers of to-day; the gay or sombre costumes from every province of Spain, some recalling the Moor and some the motley mercenaries of Lope de Figueroa; the dense and mostly silent throng which lined for miles the avenue to the church, crowding the windows with white mantillas, fringing the eaves and ridgepoles, and clustered like swarming bees on every kind of open ground; all these certainly touched the imagination, but, in my case, at least, with a chill as of the dead man's hand that played so large a part in earlier incantations to recall the buried or delay the inevitable. There was everything to remind one of the past; there was nothing to suggest the future.

And yet I am unjust. There were the young King and his bride radiant with spirit and hope, rehearsing the idyl which is charming alike to youth and age, and giving pledges, as I hope and believe, of more peaceful and prosperous years to come for a country which has had too much glory and too little good housekeeping. No one familiar with Spanish history, or who has even that superficial knowledge of her national character which is all that a foreigner is capable of acquiring, can expect any sudden or immediate regeneration. The bent of ages is not to be straightened in a day by never so many liberal constitutions, nor by the pedantic application of theories drawn from foreign experience, the result of a wholly different past.

If the ninety years since the French Revo-

More than a Mere Show

lution have taught anything, it is that institutions grow, and cannot be made to order, —that they grow out of an actual past, and are not to be conspired out of a conjectural future,—that human nature is stronger than any invention of man. How much of this lesson has been learned in Spain, it is hard to say; but if the young King apply his really acute intelligence, as those who know him best believe he will, to the conscientious exercise of constitutional powers and the steady development of parliamentary methods, till party leaders learn that an ounce of patience is worth a pound of passion, Spain may at length count on that duration of tranquility the want of which has been the chief obstacle to her material development. Looked at in this light, the pomps of the wedding festival on the 23d of last month may be something more than a mere show. Nor should it be forgotten that here it is not the idea of Law but of Power that is rooted in the consciousness of the people, and that ceremonial is the garment of Authority.

Madrid, as you know, being an improvised capital, is not the see of a bishop, and accordingly has no cathedral. The Atocha is a small church, and the ceremony there was necessarily private, thus lacking the popular *afluente* and the perspective which a building of ample proportions would have given to it. But the splendour of the costumes, especially those of the higher clergy and the heralds at arms, which are the same now as five hundred years ago, gave one the feeling that he saw the original scene of some illuminated page in Froissart. I was struck by the great number of times that the phrase *rey catolico de España* was repeated during the wedding service, and with the emphasis which the officiating prelate, the Archbishop of Toledo, seemed to lay upon the adjective, the *legal* title of Alfonso XII. being *rey constitucional.* I was struck also with the look

"El Rey Catolico"

of genuine happiness in the faces of the royal bride and bridegroom, which strongly confirmed the opinion of those who believe that the match is one of love and not of convenience.

The ceremony over, the King and Queen preceded by the Cabinet Ministers, the special ambassadors, and the grandees of Spain, and followed by other personages, all in coaches of state, drove at a footpace to the Palace, where Their Majesties received the congratulations of the Court, and afterwards passed in review the garrison of Madrid. By invitation of the President of the Council, the Foreign Legations witnessed the royal procession from the balconies of the Presidency. It was a very picturesque spectacle, and yet so comically like a scene from *Cinderella* as to have a strong flavour of unreality. It was the past coming back again, and thus typified one of the chronic maladies of Spain. There was no enthusiasm, nothing more than the curiosity of idleness which would have drawn as great a crowd to gape at the entry of a Japanese ambassador. I heard none of the shouts of which I read in some of the newspapers the next day. No inference, however, should be drawn from this as to the popularity or unpopularity of the King. The people of the capital have been promised the millenium too often, and have been too constantly disappointed to indulge in many illusions. Spain, isolated as in many respects she is, cannot help suffering in sympathy with the commercial depression of the rest of the world, and Spaniards, like the rest of mankind, look to a change of ministry for a change in the nature of things. The internal policies of the country (even if I could hope to understand them, as I am studying to do) do not come directly within my province; but it is safe to say that Spain is lucky in having her ablest recent statesman at the head of affairs, though at the cost of many

A Grand Public Reception

other private ambitions. That he has to steer according to the prevailing set of the wind is perhaps rather the necessity of his position than the fault of his inclination. Whoever has seen the breasts of the peasantry fringed with charms older than Carthage and relics as old as Rome, and those of the upper classes plastered with decorations, will not expect Spain to become conscious of the nineteenth century, and ready to welcome it, in a day.

On Thursday there was a grand public reception at the Palace, at which five thousand persons are said to have filed before Their Majesties in witness of their loyalty. All palaces since the *grand siècle* have been more or less tawdry, but that of Madrid has a certain massive dignity, and the throne-room especially has space and height enough to give proper effect to ceremonies of this kind. The young Queen wore her crown for the first time, and performed her new functions with the grace of entire self-possession. The ceremony, naturally somewhat tedious in itself, acquired more interest from the fact that the presence or absence of certain personages was an event of more or less political importance.

In the evening there was a dinner to the special ambassadors and the Diplomatic Corps, followed by a very crowded reception at the Palace of the Presidency, at which all of Madrid that has a name seemed to be present. The fine apartments were crowded until half-past two in the morning. The street on which the Palace stands (the Alcala) was so crammed for its whole length with people, that the carriages of Ministers on their way to the dinner were unable to pass. The mob (and a Madrid mob is no joke) became so threatening that foreign representatives were forced to renounce their privilege of free passage and to reach their dinners in a more roundabout and diplomatic fashion. It is to the credit of their professional ability that all arrived in

Driving through the Mob

Mr. Lowell's First Bull-Fight

season. I have seen nothing so characteristic since my arrival as the wild faces, threatening gestures and frightful imprecations of this jam of human beings, which, reasonably enough, refused to be driven over.

On Friday took place the first bull-fight, at which every inhabitant of Madrid and all foreigners commorant therein deemed it their natural right to be present. The latter, indeed, asserted that the teleological reason for the existence of legations was to supply their countrymen with tickets to this particular spectacle for nothing. Though I do not share in the belief that the sole use of a foreign minister is to save the cost of a *valet de place* to people who can perfectly well afford to pay for one, I did all I could to have my countrymen fare as well as the rest of the world. And so they did, if they were willing to buy the tickets which were for sale at every corner. The distribution of them had been performed on some principle unheard of out of Spain and apparently not understood even there, so that everybody was dissatisfied, most of all those who got them.

The day was as disagreeable as the Prince of the Powers of the Air could make it, even with special reference to a festival. A furious and bitterly cold wind discharged volleys of coarse dust, which stung like sleet, in every direction at once, and seemed always to threaten rain or snow, but unable to make up its mind as to which would be most unpleasant, decided on neither. Yet the broad avenue to the amphitheatre was continually blocked by the swarm of vehicles of every shape, size, colour, and discomfort that the nightmare of a bankrupt livery stabler could have invented. All the hospitals and prisons for decayed or condemned carriages seemed to have discharged their inmates for the day, and all found willing victims. And yet all Madrid seemed flocking toward the common magnet on foot also.

Buffeted by the Wind

Impressions of Spain

A Shocking Spectacle

I attended officially, as a matter of duty, and escaped early. It was my first bull-fight and will be my last. To me it was a shocking and brutalising spectacle in which all my sympathies were on the side of the bull. As I came out I was nearly ridden down by a mounted guard, owing to my want of any official badge. For the moment I almost wished myself the representative of Liberia. Since this dreadful day the 16,000 spectators who were so happy as to be present have done nothing but blow their noses and cough.

By far the prettiest and most interesting feature of the week was the dancing, in the *plaza de armas* before the Palace, of deputations from all the provinces of Spain, in their picturesque costumes. The dances were rather curious than graceful, and it was odd that the only one which we are accustomed to consider preëminently Spanish, the *cachucha*, was performed by two professional dancers. The rest had, however, a higher interest from their manifest antiquity and almost rudimentary characters. When the dances were over, the deputations were ranged in file, and passed in review by the King and his guests. One was struck by the general want of beauty, whether of face or form, in both sexes, and by the lowness of stature. But there was great vigour of body and the hard features had an expression of shrewdness and honesty. By far the prettiest among the women were those from Andalusia.

The same evening (Sunday) the King entertained the special ambassadors and diplomatic body at dinner, and this was followed by a reception. A dinner where one is planted between two entire strangers, and expected to be entertaining in an alien tongue, will, one may hope, be reckoned to our credit in another world. The reception had one striking and novel feature, and this was the marching past of the Madrid garrison with colored lanterns and

End of the festivities

torches. It was a spectacle of vivid picturesqueness.

Besides these hospitalities there were two performances at the opera, which I did not attend. During the whole week the city was gay with coloured hangings by day, and bright with illuminations (some of them very pretty) by night.

At last the natural order of things began again. As on all such occasions there had been long and constantly heightening expectation, short fruition, and general relief when all was over. Everybody grumbled, everybody could have managed things better; and yet on the whole, I think, everything went off almost better than could have been expected.

III

THE DEATH OF QUEEN MERCEDES

III

THE DEATH OF QUEEN MERCEDES

3 July, 1878.

AT my first interview with Mr. Silvela after my return from my furlough, he told me that the Queen was ill. Driving too late, he said, by the side of the lake in the Casa del Campo, she had taken cold; some symptoms of fever had shown themselves; there were fears lest these should assume a typhoidal character; the symptoms were complicated and the diagnosis made less easy by her being with child; as she had already miscarried once, the doctors might order her to keep her bed or a reclining-chair for months to come; naturally there was some anxiety, but her youth and

Anxiety for the Queen

A Change for the Worse

strong constitution were greatly in her favour. Mr. Silvela spoke with a great deal of feeling, but certainly did not give me the impression that the case was so very serious, much less that it was hopeless. It seemed rather to be only a question whether the Queen would be able to hold the reception which had been announced for her birthday (the 24th).

This was on the 19th of June. Two days afterward I read in the morning paper that the case was putting on a grave look, and that the physicians hitherto in attendance (all of them accoucheurs) began to fear that the real disease was gastric fever, all the more to be dreaded in the Queen's case, as one of her sisters had died of it, and one of her brothers, after lingering a year, of the weakness consequent upon an attack of it. I at once went over to the Palace to make inquiries and to inscribe my name in the book placed for the purpose in the *Mayordomia Mayor*. I did not see Mr.

Silvela, but Señor Ferraz, the under secretary, told me that the Queen's condition was alarming.

Next day the crowd of inquirers (a crowd embracing all classes) became so great that a separate register for the Diplomatic Corps was placed in the department of state, and regular bulletins began to be issued three times a day.

Up to this time the situation of the Queen could not have been considered as one of eminent danger, for the Duke and Duchess of Montpensier had not been summoned, and the patient was still attended only by the physicians already mentioned. The first consultation at which eminent practitioners from outside the Palace attended, took place on the 24th. Meanwhile, the wildest and, I may say, most atrocious rumours were current among the vulgar, so atrocious, indeed, that I will not shock you with a repetition of them.

From this time forward I went several

The Queen Passes Away

times every day to ask for news at the Palace. Even so late as Tuesday the 25th the case was not thought desperate. On that day I was assured that it was the opinion of the physicians that if the internal hemorrhage (which had been one of the worst features of the case) did not recur during the night, recovery was certain. It did not recur, but nevertheless the weakness of the sufferer became so excessive that extreme unction was administered early on the morning of Wednesday. After this there was a slight rally, followed by a rapid loss of strength and consciousness, ending in death at a quarter past twelve.

During the last few days of the Queen's illness, the aspect of the city had been strikingly impressive. It was, I think, sensibly less noisy than usual, as if it were all a chamber of death, in which the voice must be bated. Groups gathered and talked in undertone. About the Palace there was a silent crowd day and night, and there could be no question that the sorrow was universal and profound. On the last day I was at the Palace just when the poor girl was dying. As I crossed the great interior courtyard, which was perfectly empty, I was startled by a dull roar not unlike that of the vehicles in a great city. It was reverberated and multiplied by the huge cavern of the Palace court. At first I could see nothing that accounted for it, but presently found that the arched corridors all around the square were filled, both on the ground floor and the first storey, with an anxious crowd, whose eager questions and answers, though subdued to the utmost, produced the strange thunder I had heard. It almost seemed for a moment as if the Palace itself had became vocal.

At the time of the royal marriage I told you that the crowd in the streets was indifferent and silent. My own impression was confirmed by that of others. The match was certainly not popular, nor did the bride

A Thunder of Hushed Voices

Sorrow and Sympathy

call forth any marks of public sympathy. The position of the young Queen was difficult and delicate, demanding more than common tact and discretion to make it even tenable, much more, influential. On the day of her death the difference was immense. Sorrow and sympathy were in every heart and on every face. By her good temper, good sense, and womanly virtues, the girl of seventeen had not only endeared herself to those immediately about her, but had become an important factor in the destiny of Spain. I know very well what divinity doth hedge royal personages, and how truly legendary they become even during their lives, but it is no exaggeration to say that she had made herself an element of the public welfare, and that her death is a national calamity. Had she lived she would have given stability to the throne of her husband, over whom her influence was wholly for good. She was not beautiful, but the cordial simplicity of her manner, the grace of her bearing, her fine eyes, and the youth and purity of her face gave her a charm that mere beauty never attains.

Seldom has an event combined more impressive circumstances. Youth, station, love, happiness, promise, every element of hope and confidence, were present to give pathos to the sudden catastrophe. It seemed but yesterday that she had passed through the city in bridal triumph. On that day, as in most Spanish ceremonies of the kind, an empty carriage, called a *coche de respeto,* was one of the peculiar features of the procession. On the day of the funeral the *coche de respeto* was the huge vehicle (prophetically, as it should almost seem, named *de ambos mundos*), drawn by eight white horses, in which we had seen her pass a happy bride. Surely the two worlds were never more impressively brought face to face.

Grief and sympathy were universal, and with these a not unnatural anxiety about

A Pathetic Catastrophe

The Young King's Manliness

the future. The young King has borne himself with great manliness and self-restraint, though his face shows deep marks of the trial he has endured and has still to endure. The Duke and Duchess of Montpensier receive less sympathy, for, as generally on such occasions, there are not wanting those who see in the Queen's death a blow of retributive justice for the royal marriages of 1846, forgetting into how many obscure households Death may have entered on the same day and left behind him the same desolation.

One cannot help recalling the familiar stanza of Malherbe :

> " Le pauvre en sa cabane qui de chaume se couvre
>   Est sujet à ses lois,
>   Et la garde qui veille aux barrières du Louvre
>   N'en défend point nos rois."

The moment I heard of the Queen's death I sent a note to Mr. Silvela, of which a copy is annexed. I also, on receiving the President's despatch, instantly inclosed to him a copy of it. I was very glad that the President thought proper to send it, for it could not fail to be grateful, as, indeed, I am sure it has been.

To-day at noon the Diplomatic Corps were received in audiences of condolence (painfully trying on both sides) by the King, the Princess of Asturias, and the Duke and Duchess of Montpensier, with their surviving unmarried daughter. The King leaves to-morrow morning for the Escorial, where it is said he will spend a month.

On the 17th of this month a solemn mass for the repose of the late Queen's soul will be celebrated at the expense and under the direction of the Government. The other foreign ministers here have written to their respective governments, asking to be deputed as special envoys for that occasion. I shall accordingly send you a telegram asking whether, in case they should be so deputed, I should assume the same function myself.

IV

ATTEMPTED ASSASSINATION OF THE KING

IV

ATTEMPTED ASSASSINATION OF THE KING

October 29, 1878.

THE telegraph will have long ago informed you of the attempt made last Friday (25th) upon the life of the King. As the Minister of Foreign Affairs at once sent off telegrams to all Spanish ministers abroad, I did not think it necessary to send a cable dispatch.

The King was making his entry into Madrid on his return from a tour of several weeks in the northern provinces, in the course of which he had directed the autumn manœuvres of the troops at Vitoria. It was his first public appearance in Madrid since the death of his Queen on the 26th of June,

A Bullet for Alfonso

Silence of the Crowd

and it was no doubt hoped, if not expected, that the still surviving sympathy with that great calamity would communicate some of its warmth to the crowd which lined the streets through which he passed. In spite of the officially reported enthusiasm, the young monarch's reception in the north had been more than cool. His tour, so far as concerns any political effect, had been so complete a failure that the original route sketched out for him had been changed, and he forbore to visit certain towns rather than run the risk of hostile demonstrations more emphatic than silence. Perhaps Madrid would be less indifferent. Friday was a chilly and lowering day, but the profound silence of the throng which had gathered to see the pageant go by added a chill to that of the weather. The official cheers from the Government buildings but emphasised the general silence.

The King was passing along the Calle Mayor, and drawing near to the Palace.

Hitherto he had gone at a foot-pace, but now, as he said afterwards, "he began to be impatient to get home," and spurred his horse to a trot. Just as he did so, a shot was heard. The King, who showed great coolness, reined up, and faced in the direction from which it came. The would-be assassin, who had moved a few paces from where he had been standing, and had put on the air of an interested spectator, was pointed out by some women who had seen him fire, and at once arrested. No pistol was found upon him (though there were caps and cartridges in his pocket), nor has any since been traced. He is said to have fired twice, but only one ball has been found, and this had apparently rebounded after striking the house opposite. At first it was reported that a soldier had been slightly wounded; then that the ball had passed through the sleeve of his coat, and now even this seems doubtful.

The criminal is a young man named

Pardon Impossible

Oliva, a Catalonian, and by trade a cooper. He belongs to a respectable family in easy circumstances, who found it impossible to restrain his irregular tendencies, and to give him a career more suitable to their own condition in life. He at once avowed his crime, and with melodramatic dignity announced himself a socialist and member of the International. He denied having accomplices, though the disappearance of his pistol seems to imply it. It is a curious illustration of the artificial state of politics here, that, although the King would naturally be glad to pardon the criminal, it is said that he will be unable to do so lest the whole affair should seem a tragic comedy arranged beforehand between the ministry and the actors as a test of popular sentiment.

On Saturday, the 26th, the King received the felicitations of the diplomatic body. Among other things he said to me, "I almost wish he had hit me, I am so tired." Indeed, his position is a trying one, and I feel sure that if he were allowed more freely to follow his own impulses and to break through the hedge of etiquette which the conservative wing of the restoration have planted between him and his people, his natural qualities of character and temperament would make him popular.

On the same afternoon (Saturday) the King drove out with his sister the Princess of Asturias, himself holding the reins, and without guards. He was well received by the people, though the effect was dampened by the factitious enthusiasm of some soldiers, who, it is said, had been blunderingly detailed for the purpose by the captain-general of the province.

The only possible effect, or perhaps I should say consequence, of the event of Friday, would be to make the policy of the present ministry more reactionary and repressive. Already the *Politica*, the organ, as it is called, of Señor Cánovas, is urging such a course, and declaring that the

Mr. Seward's Telegram

act of Moncasi[1] is but a symptom of the general feeling of Catalonia, with which province severe measures should be taken. But the majority even of the ministerial press is more sensible and not yet ready to identify political opposition either with regicide or rebellion.

Mr. Seward's telegram directing me to convey to His Majesty the congratulations of the President and the people of the United States on his providential escape was received on Sunday morning. I at once communicated it to the Minister of State in the note of which a copy is inclosed, and on the following day received Mr. Silvela's reply, a copy and translation of which are also hereto annexed.

[1] The would-be assassin's name was Juan Oliva y Moncasi.

V

GENERAL GRANT'S VISIT TO SPAIN

V

GENERAL GRANT'S VISIT TO SPAIN

October 29, 1878.

I HAVE the honour to inform you that General Grant arrived here on the morning of the 18th. At the station he was received by the civil governor of the province, by a general and two aides-de-camp on the part of the Minister of War, and by the members of this legation. At all the stations on the road he was greeted by the local authorities. Though he arrived in Madrid on the day he originally fixed, he had entered Spain three days earlier than he intended, in compliance with an invitation of the King (received through the Spanish consul at Bordeaux) to be present at the autumn manœuvres near Vitoria.

Arrival of General Grant

Mr. Lowell dines the ex-President

General Grant while there was presented to the King, dined with him, and rode by his side during one of the reviews. He spoke in very warm terms of the excellent quality, appearance, and discipline of the Spanish troops.

During his stay here he visited the various museums, the Escorial and Toledo. To the last place I was unable to accompany him on account of an engagement to dine with the Minister of Foreign Affairs. On Saturday he and Mrs. Grant were received in private audience by the Princess of Asturias. On Monday evening they dined at my house, meeting the president of the council, the ministers of foreign affairs and of war, the civil and military governors, and the principal foreign ministers. After the dinner a reception took place, where as many persons as my house would accommodate were presented to the General and Mrs. Grant.

The next day Mr. Cánovas del Castillo

gave a great dinner in honour of General Grant at the Palace of the Presidency, after which the chief guests withdrew to the opera, where the ministerial box had been put at their disposal, and whither Mrs. Grant had gone earlier in the evening.

General Grant left Madrid on Friday, the 25th, at nine o'clock P.M., for Lisbon, the Portuguese Minister here having already telegraphed his coming in order that he should be properly received. In consequence of this latter circumstance it was impossible for him to delay his departure in order to take formal leave of the King, as he otherwise would gladly have done. I made the proper explanations and apologies to His Majesty at our reception next day.

Every possible attention and courtesy were shown to General Grant during his stay by the Spanish Government, and the Minister for Foreign Affairs took occasion to tell me that these civilities were intended not only to show respect and good will to

Significant Civilities

General Grant, but to the Government and people of the United States.

General Grant several times expressed to me very warmly his pleasure and satisfaction at the manner in which he had been received and treated. Both he and Mrs. Grant spoke repeatedly of the great enjoyment they had had in their visit.

From Portugal General Grant goes to Cadiz, and thence to Malaga. From Malaga he will visit Granada, Cordova, and Seville, going thence to Gibraltar. Mr. Silvela begged me to keep him informed of the General's movements in Spain, in order that the necessary orders might be given for his fitting reception everywhere by the public authorities.

VI

THE KING'S SECOND MARRIAGE

VI

THE KING'S SECOND MARRIAGE

16 November, 1879.

Maria Christina

I HAVE the honour to enclose copy and translation of the official note communicating the intended marriage of the King, and also a copy of my reply.

Naturally this event does not excite either the sympathies or the animosities awakened by the wedding of twenty-two months ago, and it occurs at a time when the country is saddened by the terrible inundations of Murcia, and public attention distracted by the recent news from Cuba. The young Archduchess is said to possess qualities likely to render her popular, if only she is able to disarm the criticism to which any foreign and perhaps especially

No Political Significance

any Austrian princess will be exposed in Spain.

The match is declared to have no political significance whatever, though circumstances may easily be imagined in which the eagerness of many Spaniards that Spain should follow the example of Italy under the leadership of Cavour might guide it in an importance which it does not intrinsically possess.

15 December, 1879.

I have not deemed it necessary to trouble you with any details of the royal wedding, which differed in no respect from that of two years ago, fully described in my despatch at the time. The only notable difference was the presence of the Queen Mother, who naturally absented herself from the former ceremony, in which a daughter of the brother-in-law who had been the main instrument of her dethronement was the bride.

It is a curious fact that the ex-Queen was received wherever she showed herself in public with the most noisy demonstrations of popularity, in marked contrast with the silence with which her son and his Austrian bride were received. This was partly, no doubt, intended to heighten the emphasis of the public indifference toward them, but it was also a proof of her personal popularity, which is still very great in spite of all her faults and follies, and perhaps it might be said in consequence of them.

I do not mention this as having the least political significance, but only as a fact worth recording, and as another proof that the very qualities or defects of character which make those that are marked by them bad rulers, are a large constituent in the affection with which they are regarded by the unthinking. The father of Isabel II., one of the basest men and worst kings that ever lived, was always popular, mainly because he contrived to pass off as careless

Ex-Queen Isabella's Popularity

An Attractive Personality

good humour the cynical want of feeling with which he perpetrated his treacheries, perjuries, and cruelties.

The new Queen attracts sympathy by the gracious cordiality of her manners, her youth, and the dignity of her bearing. She is good-looking without being beautiful; she has the projecting chin of her race, though softened in her by feminine delicacy of feature. One seems to see in her a certain resemblance to Marie Antoinette, and she mounts a throne that certainly seems less firm than that of France when her kinswoman arrived in Paris to share what all believed would be the prosperous fortunes of its heir-apparent. Such associations lent a kind of pathos to the unaffected happiness which lighted the face of Maria Christina.

INDEX

Adee, A. A., iv, 19
Alfonso XII., v, vi, 5, 13-15; education, 36; congratulations to, 56; first wedding, 58 *et seq.*; bereavement, 82, 83; attempted assassination, 87 *et seq.*; second marriage, 101 *et seq.*
Alfonso XIII., 15
Asturias, Princess of, 83, 91, 96
Atocha, The, 63

Broglie, Duke of, 54
Bull-fight, 68

Campos, Martinez de (Marshal), 8, 11
Cánovas del Castillo, Antonio, 14, 28-37, 39, 91, 96
Carlos (Don), 27
Castelar, Emilio, 7, 29, 38
Censorship, 40, 41
Century Magazine, 15
Cushing, Caleb (Minister), 4, 9, 11

Dana, Henrietta C., 15
Dances, national, 70

Ellen Rizpah, Rising Sun, and *Edward Lee* (whaling vessels), vi
Empleomania, 26

Figueras, Estanislao, 6

Grant, U. S., vi, 95-98

Hayes, President, 44, 49, 56, 57, 82
Herrera, Posada, 37

Irving, Washington, vii, 4, 11
Isabel II. (ex-Queen), 5, 41, 102, 103

La Granja, v, 13
La Torre, Duke of. *See* Serrano

Madrid Society of Political Economy, 45
Malherbe, 82
Maria Cristina (Queen), vii, 15, 101
Mercedes (Queen), vii, 13, 15, 53, 54 ; death, 75 *et seq.*
Merelo, Manuel, 41
Moncasi, Juan Oliva y, 16, 90, 92
Montpensier, Duke of, 53 ; and Duchess, 77, 82, 83

Pavia (General), 8
Pedregal (President), 10
Pi y Margall, Francisco, 7

Reed, Dwight, vii
Republicanism, 39
Royalists, 27

Salmeron, Nicolas, 7
Serrano, General (Duke of La Torre), 5, 8, 38
Seward, William H., Secretary of State, 92
Sickles, Daniel E. (Minister), 4, 11
Silvela, Manuel, iv, 46, 50, 82

Spain's friendliness toward United States, vi ; domestic politics, 23 *et seq.* ; custom-houses, 43 ; sensitiveness, 48

Spanish marriages, 53

Tariff as a weapon, 42 *et seq.*
Tetuan, Duke of, 49, 50
Tonnage duty on Spanish vessels, 44
Treaty of commerce proposed, 47

Virginius affair, 11

Zanjon, truce of, 11

www.ingramcontent.com/pod-product-compliance
Lightning Source LLC
Chambersburg PA
CBHW020133170426
43199CB00010B/729